Phrawg Phables

Wonderings and Wanderings

told by
Michael S. Pritchard

Buttonwood Press
2007

Pritchard, Michael S.
    Phrawg phables: Wonderings and wanderings. Haslett, Mich.: Buttonwood
Press, 2007.
    viii,94 pp.
    1. Thought and thinking   2. Memory   1. Title

J 153.42 P75

ISBN: 978-0-9742920-7-6

Layout, cover design and illustrations by LanWord
Printed by Fidlar Doubleday, Inc.

To my grandchildren,
Ryan and Kyra

Contents

I

Phrawg

Phrawg lived in a big house with two giants and three cats. He sat all day long in a rocking chair.

He was as big as a cat, his eyes bigger than marbles, and his mouth as wide as his head. The cats liked to take naps in the rocking chair. But when they saw Phrawg, they were frightened.

Phrawg wore a tag that said he was a *puppet toad*. But he was green. Toads are brown and not nearly so big, he thought.

The giants called him a frog. "Maybe I *am* a frog," Phrawg thought. But he knew he was too big to be an ordinary frog. Besides, he had never jumped.

"Still," reflected Phrawg, "I know I'm *something*. In fact, I seem to be something *like* a frog—only much, much bigger. . .and smarter. Maybe I'm a little bit like a toad, too—a really, really big one, and a green one as well. I can call myself whatever I want. Neither frog nor toad, but a little like each, my name will be *Phrawg*."

Phrawg tried to pay attention to everything around him. He listened to the giants talking with each other. At first, they were hard to understand—and *very* loud. After a while, they were easy to understand—but they were still *very* loud.

Phrawg watched the cats wander in and out of the big room where he stayed. He listened to them, too. They talked to each other just like the giants did, only *very* softly.

The giants couldn't hear the cats unless they shouted. But when the cats shouted, everything sounded like "Meow," to the giants. So, they could only guess what the cats were trying to say. Sometimes it took them a long, long time—and many, many meows.

Although he never moved about on his own, Phrawg thought a lot about what he saw and heard. He also had lots of questions. Where do those cats go when they leave this room? What do they do when they aren't here? Where do the giants go? What do they do when they aren't here? Why do those cats look out the window so much? Where was I before I was here? How did I get here?

It was difficult for Phrawg to think clearly about these questions when the giants were in the room. They were much too noisy. When they left, Phrawg was usually quite relieved. "At last," he sighed, "I can hear myself think."

Phrawg knew why the giants had put him on the rocking chair. It was to scare the cats away. The giants thought that only giants should sit in the rocking chair—except for Phrawg. Of course, to the cats, Phrawg seemed to be a giant, too. So, naturally they were afraid to jump up on the rocking chair when he was there.

However, one day a giant picked up Phrawg and carried him over to the couch. Phrawg knew that this was the cats' favorite napping place. He wondered what they'd do when they noticed he was on the couch. Soon he would find out.

II

Cat Talk

"Meow, meow, meow!!!" Hobbes, Tweetie, and Ms. Josie shouted as loudly as they could. They heard footsteps approaching the kitchen. But there still was no food in their dishes.

"Meow, meow, meow!!!" they repeated.

"What's with those giants?" asked Ms. Josie. "They don't seem to understand us at all."

"They're okay," replied Hobbes. "You just have to keep shouting it again and again—food, food, food. Eventually they hear us."

"But it isn't just food," protested Ms. Josie. "They don't seem to understand anything we say—even when we shout at the top of our lungs."

"Right," said Tweetie. "When I say *Meow* I mean one thing. When I say *Meoow* I mean another. And when I say *Meooow* I mean yet another. But it all seems to be the same to those giants."

"Well," agreed Hobbes, "I suppose you are right about that. We've been trying to get them to understand us for more than 15 years. It took us a while to catch on to what they say, but now it's pretty easy."

"But it's also pretty silly," said Ms. Josie. "They say, 'Nice kitty. Good kitty. Bad kitty. Hobbes, why don't you sit in my lap for a while. Oh, Tweetie, you're so cute,' and on and on and on."

"You'd think that by now they'd understand us," said Tweetie.

"There's another thing," added Ms. Josie, "I really don't like all the nicknames they've given us—Josie-Bell, J.B., Jelly-Bean, Jelly-Belly. I keep telling them, 'Call me Ms. Josie, if you please.' But they just don't get it."

"That's not so bad," replied Hobbes. "How would you like to be called Hobble, Hobble-Toes, or Toes? What's wrong with plain old *Hobbes*?"

"I kind of like being called Tweet and Tweetie-Pie," said Tweetie. "But

Tweeters makes me mad."

"Worse than all those nicknames," said Hobbes, "is all the baby-talk. 'Are you little babies hungry?' Duh, what do you think we've been telling you for the last 15 minutes?"

"Or how about, 'See you little babies later,' when they go out the door?" added Ms. Josie. *"Babies!* We're *old.* Isn't it about time they started treating us with a little respect?"

"Oh, they talk that way because they think we're so sweet and cuddly," said Tweetie.

"Sweet and cuddly," replied Ms. Josie. "That's another thing. I'll cuddle when *I* want to—not when some giant tries to pick me up and squeeze my tummy. Sometimes I just want to be left alone."

"Yes," said Hobbes, "and I do wish they'd quit shouting all the time. They make my ears hurt. Why don't they talk normally like we do?"

"Because then they couldn't hear each other," said Ms. Josie. "I think they're hard of hearing. They don't even notice that we talk to each other."

"Yes," agreed Tweetie, "they seem to think that all we do is scream, *Meow.* If only they could hear what we're saying right now. But they can't."

"Right," added Ms. Josie. "I try politely telling them that I need some peace and quiet so that I can take a nap. They act like they don't hear me at all. So, I yell at them. But then they pick me up and shout all that baby talk at me. Yuck!"

"Speaking of naps," said Hobbes, "how about that stuffed toad on the rocking chair? What's he doing there, anyway? That's one of my napping spots."

"Well," said Ms. Josie, "I heard one of the giants say that if the toad were on the rocking chair, none of us would be brave enough to jump up there and take a nap."

"That's certainly true," admitted Hobbes. "That toad looks mean—and hungry. He just sits there with his mouth wide open. Have you noticed how *big* his mouth is?"

"Yes," said Tweetie, "and he has eyes bigger than marbles—just staring at you."

"Phooey on the rocking chair," scoffed Hobbes. "I prefer the couch anyway. That's the best place for naps—except when the sun is shining. Then the floor in front of the sliding glass doors is best."

"Right," said Ms. Josie. "Those sliding glass doors are great. You can see all the birds out on the porch. I just wish someone would open those doors for us. It'd be fun to play with the birds—especially those red ones."

"You actually made it out there once, Tweetie, remember?" said Hobbes.

"No, I don't remember that," said Tweetie.

"I thought the giants were going to chase you right off the porch—9 feet to the ground," said Hobbes. "Luckily, you just ran back into the house."

"I don't remember that," said Tweetie. "Where was I?"

"You were on the porch, Tweetie," said Ms. Josie. "Then you ran back into the house."

"Oh," said Tweetie.

"Watch out!" shouted Ms. Josie. She hissed at a large black and white cat that the giants had let in the house.

"Hsss-s-s-s," whispered Hobbes.

"Hsss-s-s-s," echoed Tweetie.

"Ginger!" shouted one of the giants. "Behave yourself, Ginger. Don't pick on those poor kitties."

"You tell her, giant," said Ms. Josie. "Get that stupid cat out of here. I'd whack her in the nose if I had any claws. Go get her, Hobbes."

"**Hsss-s-s-s**," said Hobbes, Ms. Josie, and Tweetie together. Ginger ran away.

"You know," said Hobbes, "Ginger understands *hsss-s-s-s* all right. But when the giants say, 'Leave them alone, Ginger. Don't be mean,

Ginger,' it must sound to her like, 'Blah, blah, blah, Ginger. Blah, blah, blah, Ginger.' I think she barely recognizes her own name. Everything else is blah, blah, blah."

"Giants and cats," grumbled Ms. Josie. "Talk about dumb—except for us, of course."

"Of course," agreed Hobbes.

"Of course," nodded Tweetie.

18

III

Hobbes

Hobbes was a cat who thought she was a tiger. Every morning she walked around the house to make sure everything was just the way she wanted it to be. This morning she finished her walk, yawned and jumped onto the couch.

"Philibit," spouted Phrawg.

"Y-o-w-w-l-l-l!!!" shouted Hobbes.

"Pipe down phuzz ball . . . You're hurting my ears."

"I'm not a fuzz ball. I'm a tiger, you stuffed toad."

"I'm not a stuffed toad. In fact, I'm not a toad at all. I'm a phrawg."

"Hssssss."

"Philibit."

"*Philibit?* What does that mean?"

"It means that I want to be left alone," said Phrawg. "Just what does *hsssss* mean?"

"It means that if you come any closer, you'll be sorry," said Hobbes.

"Believe me, I don't want to get any closer to you," insisted Phrawg. "I told you I want to be left alone."

"Well, what makes you think a tiger would want to hang around with a toad who thinks he's a frog?"

"I said *phrawg*, not *frog*. Spell that 'p-h-r-a-w-g,' please."

"I've never heard of such a thing—a *phrawg*?" asked Hobbes. "What's that?"

"A big thinker," replied Phrawg.

"Well, you're big all right—a big toad," said Hobbes.

"I'm too big to be a toad," objected Phrawg. "Why, I'm as big as you are."

"I can see that," said Hobbes. "I must admit that I've never seen such a big toad. And you certainly talk more than any toad I've ever seen before."

"That's because I have lots of thoughts," said Phrawg. "And here's one of them. You're too small to be a tiger. You are a cat."

"Tigers are cats. Cats come in many sizes. So, why can't tigers come in many sizes?" asked Hobbes. "I'm a small-sized tiger."

"You are a tiger *cat*, not a tiger," corrected Phrawg. "You might look like a tiny tiger, but you're just a cat."

"Well, if you can call yourself a phrawg, I can call myself a tiger," said Hobbes. She jumped off the couch and began to walk away.

"Wait a minute, phuzzy," demanded Phrawg. "Where do you think you're going?"

"I'm going for a walk," replied Hobbes. "But why should you care? I thought you wanted to be alone."

"Well, I've changed my mind." said Phrawg. "You seem quite confused, and I specialize in thinking clearly. Maybe I can help you out."

"I don't need any help," insisted Hobbes. "You're the one who's confused. You think you're a phrawg, but you're just a stuffed toad who sits around all day . . . ."

"You still haven't answered my question," interrupted Phrawg. "Where do you think you're going?"

"I told you, I'm going for a walk."

"But *where* are you going? What is your *destination*?"

"My destination? I don't have one. I'm just taking a walk."

"Oh, you have to have a destination. Otherwise you'll never get where you're going."

"But if I'm not going anywhere, there's nowhere I need to get to."

"Then you'll just keep going and going and going—and getting nowhere."

"I can walk until I'm tired of walking. Then I can stop and talk with my sisters."

"Well then, that's you're destination," concluded Phrawg. "Wherever you stop is your destination."

"I'm not taking a walk so that I can see my sisters," insisted Hobbes. "I'm taking a walk just for the fun of it. Then I'll stop and see my sisters."

"Taking a walk for the fun of it. I don't get it. How can taking a walk without a destination be fun?"

"You'll never know if you just sit there all day."

"Maybe not. But that's not important. I have more important things to do—right here."

"More important things to do? Like what?"

"Like *thinking*," said Phrawg. "I told you I'm a big thinker."

"Well, I'm a big walker," huffed Hobbes, as she walked into the next room.

IV

A Philosophical Phrawg

Hobbes hoped that Phrawg would be gone by the time she returned to the couch. "But how could he be if all he does is sit around thinking?" thought Hobbes. "What on earth does he think about? If he's still there when I get back, I'll ask him."

Sure enough, Phrawg was still curled up on the couch. "You just sit there thinking all day and night?" hissed Hobbes. "Thinking about what? If you never get out and about, how can you have anything to think about?”

“Ideas. I have ideas to think about.”

“Ideas? Where do they come from? Inside your big head?”

“Yup.”

“How did you get on my couch, anyway?” asked Hobbes. “I thought you were on the rocking chair.”

“I have no idea how I got here,” admitted Phrawg. “But now that I’m here, I’m staying.”

“Hsss, hsss.”

"I told you I have no interest in getting any closer to you."

"You aren't listening very carefully. I said *hsss, hsss,* not *hsss-s-s-s.*"

"It all sounds the same to me. Would you please speak more plainly?"

"Okay. Get off my couch, toad. Is that plain enough for you?"

"*Your* couch? Look, phuzz ball, I'm not moving. This couch is as much mine as it is yours."

"I told you I'm not a fuzz ball. I'm a tiger, and I've been living in this house a lot longer than you have."

"You're no tiger. You're a cat—a little house cat."

"Look at my stripes, toad."

"You're a tiger *cat*. You might have stripes, but you aren't big enough to be a tiger. And I told you I'm not a toad. My name is Phrawg."

"I don't care what your name is. You're too big to be a frog. You're just a stuffed toad."

"Tell me, can a toad be as big as a tiger? I'm as big as you are."

"Well, I don't think a *real* toad can be as big as even a little cat. I said you are a *stuffed* toad. You're not even a *real* toad."

"Of course I'm not a real toad. I'm a phrawg—a *real* phrawg."

"Well, I suppose you're a real something. But whatever that is, it can't amount to much. All you do is sit around all day and night."

"Yes, I do. But I'm very busy."

"Busy? Busy doing what?"

"Thinking. I told you I'm a big thinker. In fact, I'm a very philosophical phrawg."

"A philosophical phrawg? Who ever heard of such a thing?"

"I dare say, you haven't. First, you don't even recognize a phrawg when you see one. Second, I doubt very much that you have any idea of what it means to be philosophical."

"Well, you're right about that."

"Whether you know it or not, I *am* a phrawg. That's plain to see. Get used to it. I'm a philosophical phrawg because I'm searching for wisdom."

"Okay Mr. Wise Guy, that's enough for now," shrugged Hobbes. "I'm off for a walk." And, with that, Hobbes jumped off the couch and ran out of the room.

V

Tweetie

Hobbes returned from her walk around the house and jumped onto the couch. Once again, she hoped that Phrawg wasn't there. But there he was. He still hadn't moved.

"Well, well, here's the cat who thinks she has no destination." croaked Phrawg. "But here you are. So, *this* must be your destination."

"Very funny, Phrawg," yawned Hobbes. "For your information, this is where I take my naps."

"Naps? I don't have time for naps," replied Phrawg. "Thinking is a full time job."

"Get serious," said Hobbes. "If you just sit in one place all the time, you can't have much to think about. And it has to be pretty boring."

"It's not boring at all," objected Phrawg. "You should try it and see for yourself."

"Well, you should try taking a walk. Then you might find a thing or two worth thinking about."

"You first, phuzzy. Sit still for a while and try a little thinking."

"About what?"

"Well, you could think about thinking," suggested Phrawg. "Do you realize what a wonderful thing thinking is?"

"What on earth do you mean? Think about *thinking*?"   Hobbes looked around the room. "I can think about that lamp over there. I can think about the fireplace, the carpet, the rocking chairs, the window, the birds in the trees, the squirrels chasing each other, but . . . ."

"My, my, you are stubborn, aren't you?" said Phrawg. "Stop looking all around you. That only makes it harder. Shut your eyes for a moment, and forget about all those other things. Then just sit quietly and think about the fact that you are still thinking."

Hobbes shut her eyes and tried to stop thinking about the lamp, the fireplace, the carpet, the rocking chairs, the birds, and the squirrels. Instead, she thought about her sister, Tweetie. "Poor Tweetie," thought Hobbes. "She can hardly remember anything any more." Thinking about this made Hobbes very sad, and she began to cry.

"Why are you crying?" Phrawg asked softly.

"Phrawg," said Hobbes, "my sister Tweetie has a very bad memory and sometimes gets quite confused. She walks around the house every day as if she's never been there before. Each time she sees the soft chair in the basement she says, 'What a wonderful place to take a nap. I've never seen such a cozy little spot.' Sometimes she asks me when I'll take her home. I tell her that this is our home. But she doesn't seem to believe me. I'd like to help her, but I'm not sure how I can."

"Well," said Phrawg, "I wish I could help you, but I'm not at all sure what it's like to be so forgetful. My memory is quite good, you know."

"So is mine," said Hobbes. "But I have to try to help her. Would you walk with us around the house today? Then you'll see what I mean about poor Tweetie."

"Well, I guess I could do that," replied Phrawg.

So Hobbes and Phrawg went off together to take a walk with Tweetie. They found her in the big room in the basement waiting for Hobbes.

"Oh, there you are," purred Tweetie. "I was wondering where you were."

"We're here to go for a walk with you," said Hobbes.

"I'm ready," said Tweetie.

"This is Phrawg. He'd like to join us."

"Let's go, then," said Tweetie.

44

VI

A Walk

Hobbes and Tweetie took the same walk every day. First they stopped in a corner and looked for the house mouse.

"Smells mousy to me," said Tweetie. "I've never smelled such a mousy smell before," she added.

"She says that every day," Hobbes whispered to Phrawg.

Suddenly the house mouse jumped in front of Tweetie, who was so startled that she lept straight up in the air.

"Hah!" exclaimed the mouse. "Scaredy cat, scaredy cat, can't catch a mouse. Chase me. Chase me, all around the house." And with that the little mouse quickly scampered away.

"Let's get it! Let's get it," shouted Tweetie, as she ran after the mouse. But Hobbes didn't move. Instead, she said to Phrawg, "Tweetie will be right back, and she won't even remember chasing that mouse. So, that's no fun."

"Look out the window at those birds," said Tweetie as she walked back into the room. "There's a red one, a blue one, and . . . and the blue sky is beautiful. See what I mean? Look at that dog."

"What's that dog have to do with the birds or the blue sky?" Hobbes asked Tweetie.

"That dog ran away from home and that crow is the biggest bird I've ever seen. And look at that truck going by. It's going much too fast to . . . ," Tweetie paused for a moment. Then she continued, ". . . two, three, four, five, six bees are buzzing around the flowers. Look at that buzzing bee . . . Be quiet . . . Should I be quiet? Am I talking too much?"

"No, you're not talking too much," said Hobbes; but she found it hard to figure out just what Tweetie was trying to say.

"Oh, look at that," said Hobbes, stopping to look at a book on the table. "*Tales of Whales*. I'll bet that's really interesting."

"Tales of wails. How sad," said Tweetie, and she kept on walking. "I don't like stories about crying."

"Oh, no, Tweetie. It's not about crying at all."

"I know that," said Tweetie, with a twinkle in her eye.

"It's stories about whales swimming in the ocean," explained Hobbes.

"What whales?"

"Whales in the book."

"What book?"

"The book on the table, the one we just saw on the table."

"I don't remember that. Where was I?"

"Right here, with me."

"Well, I'm glad you're with me," said Tweetie. "I don't like being alone."

They walked into the hallway, went around the corner, and stepped into the laundry room.

"Ahh-h," sighed Tweetie, "smell those clean clothes. I've never smelled such clean clothes before."

"Yes," agreed Hobbes, "they do smell very clean."

Tweetie jumped into a basket filled with dirty clothes. "Yoosh. This is disgusting. These clothes need washing."

"There's some soap," said Hobbes, tipping over a large box of powdery soap.

"Is that snow?" asked Tweetie.

"No, just detergent," said Hobbes.

"The third gent?" teased Tweetie. "I see that big toad, but where are the other two?"

"*Deter-gent*, not a *gent*. It's laundry soap," explained Hobbes. "Besides, Phrawg doesn't like being called a toad."

"A toad's not a frog," said Tweetie. "And a frog isn't a dog, and that's because that dog outside is barking at the squirrels. Hear it barking?"

Tweetie jumped off the pile of dirty laundry, returned to the hallway, turned the corner, and went back into the big room.

As they approached the table where they had seen the book *Tales of Whales*, Tweetie looked up and said, "We don't have to stop here."

"Right," agreed Hobbes. "We can go by it."

"Buy it?" asked Tweetie, with a mischievous grin on her face. "Why would we want to buy that book?"

"I mean we can pass it and not stop at all."

"Pass it? Why would we want to throw it?"

"We wouldn't. It's a book, and books are for reading, not throwing. What I meant is that we don't have to stop. We can go right past it."

"Go right past what?"

"The book."

"What book?"

"The book, *Tales of Whales*."

"Whales have tails?"

"Yes, they do. But that's not what the book is about."

"What book?"

"*Tales of Whales.*"

"Oh, those sad stories. I don't like all that crying."

"The whales aren't crying," said Hobbes. "Nobody's crying. We've just had a nice walk, haven't we?"

"Oh, are we going to take a walk?" asked Tweetie. "That would be nice. I'm ready."

"No," said Hobbes. "We just took a walk."

"We did? I don't remember," said Tweetie. "Where was I?"

"Right here, with me," said Hobbes. "And with Phrawg."

"What frog?" asked Tweetie.

"Right here, next to you," said Hobbes.

"Oh," replied Tweetie, "the big toad."

"I'm not a toad," said Phrawg. "I'm a phrawg."

"We need to go back upstairs now," said Hobbes. "Phrawg and I are tired and need to take a nap."

"But I don't want to be alone," said Tweetie.

"You won't be," comforted Hobbes. "Here comes Ms. Josie."

"Oh, good," said Tweetie. "Maybe we can go for a walk together. I haven't had one yet today."

Quite exhausted, Hobbes and Phrawg returned to the couch, jumped up, and shut their eyes.

VII

More Talk

Hobbes opened her eyes and saw Phrawg staring at her expectantly.

"Well," said Hobbes, "see what I mean?"

"See what you mean?" asked Phrawg. "What *do* you mean?"

"See how much trouble Tweetie has remembering things?"

"Who's Tweetie?" asked Phrawg.

"Tweetie's my sister, Phrawg," replied Hobbes. "Don't you remember? You just met her on our walk around the . . . ."

"What walk?" asked Phrawg. "I've just been sitting here on the couch, like I always do."

"Oh, no!" cried Hobbes. "You can't remember things either."

"On the contrary," insisted Phrawg. "I have an excellent memory. In fact, I distinctly remember you lying there snoring just a moment ago."

"I don't snore," Hobbes protested.

"Oh, you do. Indeed, you do," said Phrawg. "Gently, but it's definitely a snore."

"But don't you remember getting off the couch with me to go see my poor sister, Tweetie?" asked Hobbes.

"I don't remember *ever* walking," said Phrawg. "So I could hardly have walked with you just a moment ago. You must have been dreaming."

"Dreaming?" puzzled Hobbes. "But it all seemed so real. It was just like all the other walks I take with Tweetie—except that, this time, you came along too."

"Well, tell me about this dream, little kitty," said Phrawg.

Hobbes told Phrawg about walking around the basement with Tweetie.

"Did she have fun?" asked Phrawg.

"Well, how could she? She can't remember anything for more than a moment," said Hobbes.

"Tell me, Hobbes," said Phrawg, "what was the best meal you ate last year?"

"How should I know?" asked Hobbes. "I don't remember meals I ate that long ago."

"I'm not surprised," replied Phrawg. "But does that mean you didn't enjoy the best meal you ate last year?"

"Of course not," insisted Hobbes. "If it was my best meal, I *must* have enjoyed it."

"Even though you don't remember what it was?" asked Phrawg.

"Yes . . . , yes, even though I don't remember it," admitted Hobbes. "I just told you that."

"Well," concluded Phrawg, "if you enjoyed something you don't remember, why can't Tweetie?"

"I . . . I don't know," admitted Hobbes. "Maybe she can."

"See what a little thinking can do for you," said Phrawg. "It can make you think even more."

"But," reflected Hobbes, "I don't see how Tweetie can enjoy the same things again and again and again. How boring that must be."

"But if she doesn't remember doing something before," asked Phrawg, "how can she be bored by doing it again? Isn't it always like doing it for the very first time?"

Hobbes had to admit she hadn't thought of that before.

"Besides," added Phrawg, "maybe Tweetie remembers more than you think she does. Take that mousy smell you mentioned. Doesn't she *always* call it a mousy smell?"

"Yes," agreed Hobbes.

"Well," said Phrawg, "does she ever say she smells a rat?"

"Oh, she'd yowl if she thought it was a rat," said Hobbes. "She doesn't like rats at all."

"So, she knows the difference between mice and rats?"

"Yes," said Hobbes, "I guess she does."

"So," suggested Phrawg, "even though she forgets lots of things, she must remember a lot, too?"

"Yes, but each time she says she's never smelled anything so mousy before," said Hobbes, "even though she smelled it just moments before."

"But she calls it a *mousy* smell, doesn't she?" repeated Phrawg. "Doesn't she remember what a mousy smell is like, even though she doesn't remember having smelled it just moments before?"

"I guess she does," agreed Hobbes.

"And can't she have fun chasing the mouse, even if she doesn't remember chasing it before?"

"Yes," said Hobbes, "She *loves* chasing the mouse."

"How about you?" asked Phrawg. "Do you love chasing the mouse?"

"Sometimes."

"But only when you remember having chased it before?"

"No," Hobbes replied. "I don't even think about having chased it before. I just chase it."

"Well," concluded Phrawg, "then you and Tweetie should be able to have fun *together*, just chasing the mouse."

"Why, yes, you are right," said Hobbes. "And we can have fun jumping on the piles of clothes, looking at the birds, the dog, and the blue sky."

"Even if Tweetie says she's never done these things before?" asked Phrawg.

"Even then," replied Hobbes.

"Even if next time she won't remember it either?" asked Phrawg.

"Even then," said Hobbes, as she jumped off the couch and ran out of the room. Phrawg heard her shout, "Hey, Ms. Josie, let's go take a walk with Tweetie!"

VIII

Ms. Josie

"I see you've been talking with that stupid stuffed toad," said Ms. Josie to Hobbes.

"He says he's a phrawg, not a toad," replied Hobbes. "Actually, he's quite smart."

"If he's so smart," said Ms. Josie, "how come he spends all his time just sitting around doing nothing?"

"He says he's so busy thinking that he doesn't have time to move around," said Hobbes.

"*Thinking?* Thinking about what?" asked Ms. Josie.

"Well, he says he's a philosophical phrawg and that he has lots of ideas to think about," said Hobbes.

"*Philosophical?*" asked Ms. Josie. "What's that supposed to mean?"

"I'm not sure," said Hobbes. "He says he's philosophical because he's searching for wisdom."

"*Searching* for wisdom by *sitting* on a couch?" asked Ms. Josie. "If I'm searching for something, I sniff all around the house until I find what

I'm looking for. What exactly does *he* do?"

"You should talk with him and see for yourself," said Hobbes.

"I think I'll do just that," said Ms. Josie. She ran into the big room and jumped up on the couch.

"Gul-lup!" shouted Phrawg.

"Gul-lup?" replied Ms. Josie. "What's that supposed to mean?"

"It means, *Who are you?*" said Phrawg.

"I'm Hobbes' sister, Ms. Josie. She says you are searching for wisdom."

"Yes," said Phrawg, "I am, indeed."

"Well," said Ms. Josie, "what makes you think you'll find wisdom *here* on this couch?"

"It doesn't really matter *where* I am," replied Phrawg. "What matters is *what* I'm thinking, no matter where I am."

"But don't you have to have something to think *about*?" puzzled Ms. Josie. "Like mice? I don't see any mice around here. If I'd never gone down into the basement, I'd never have seen any. So, how could I think about them if I'd never been off this couch?"

"I can think about mice because Hobbes told me about the house mouse," said Phrawg. "But I've plenty to think about without bothering myself about mice."

"Like what?" asked Ms. Josie.

"Like *thinking*." Pausing to scratch his chin, Phrawg continued. "I wonder how many kinds of thinking there are. Like *wondering*. That's a way of thinking. And *guessing* . . . and *figuring things out* . . . and *believing* . . . and *doubting* . . . and *remembering* . . . and . . . ."

"Okay, okay, that's enough," said Ms. Josie. "*Remembering*. That's something worth thinking about. My sister Tweetie has been having lots of problems with that."

"I know," said Phrawg. "Hobbes and I have talked about that."

"Hobbes says that you think Tweetie can still have fun even if she can't remember things. How can she?" asked Ms. Josie.

"Ah," said Phrawg, "I didn't say Tweetie can't remember *anything* at all. Maybe she remembers more than you think she does."

"Well, she doesn't seem to remember anything for more than a moment," said Ms. Josie.

"Does she remember her name?"

"Yes."

"And your name?"

"Yes."

"And does she remember where the house mouse likes to hide?"

"Yes, but she doesn't remember the last time she chased the mouse, not even a moment later."

"Do you remember the *first* time you chased the mouse?"

"The very first time?"

"Yes, the very first time."

"Well, it was . . . ummm . . . well, no, I don't, except that it was a long time ago."

"Do you think you enjoyed chasing it the first time?"

"I suppose I did. I know I do now. But I can't remember."

"But if you enjoyed it the *first* time, that wasn't because you remembered doing it before."

"True."

"And if you enjoy it now, that's not because you remember enjoying the first time."

"That's true, too."

"When Tweetie chases the mouse, does she think it's a rat, or a squirrel, or another cat?"

"No, she knows it's a mouse."

"Because she remembers what a mouse looks and smells like?"

"I'm not sure why. Maybe it's just that she's always known what a mouse looks and smells like."

"Could she forget this? Some day might she see a mouse and say, 'What's that? I've never seen anything like that before.'"

"Well, I suppose she could."

"So, can we say that *so far* she still remembers what a mouse looks and smells like?"

"It seems so."

"If we asked her whether a mouse looks like a horse, what would she say?"

"She'd say, no."

"Has she always known that?"

"No, first she had to learn what a mouse is and what a horse is, and see that they are different."

"And she hasn't forgotten that they aren't the same?"

"Right."

"So, it seems that there are lots of things Tweetie remembers."

"True," admitted Ms. Josie, "but there is so much that she forgets."

"Right," said Phrawg. "But she remembers enough that she can still have fun—chasing mice, looking at birds, dogs, and the blue sky, and spending time doing these things with you and Hobbes."

"Even though she doesn't remember the last time we'd did them together?" asked Ms. Josie.

"Even though she doesn't remember the last time—and you don't remember the first time," concluded Phrawg.

IX

Another Walk

"I see why you think Phrawg is smart," Ms. Josie said to Hobbes.

"Yes," agreed Hobbes. "He's certainly helped us with Tweetie."

"But does he really think he can find wisdom just sitting on a couch," asked Ms. Josie. "Why doesn't he get up and move around like we do? There's so much more he could see and do."

"I don't know," said Hobbes. "Why don't we ask him?"

So, Ms. Josie and Hobbes jumped onto the couch right next to Phrawg. It surprised Phrawg to have both of them beside him at once. But he seemed pleased.

"Phrawg," began Hobbes, "you say you are searching for wisdom. But this couch is so small, and there is so much to explore around the house."

"Yes," added Ms. Josie, "don't you think it would help to walk around and see other things, too?"

"Not really," said Phrawg. "As I said before, there's quite enough to keep me busy right here."

"You might keep busy with your ideas," said Hobbes, "but how do you know you have all the right kinds of ideas to help you find wisdom?"

"Right," agreed Ms. Josie. "Maybe if you walked around the house with us, you'd get some *new* ideas—ideas that aren't like any you've had before."

"Perhaps," said Phrawg. "But I'd have less time to think. I can't do two things at once, you know. If I think, I can't walk. If I walk, I can't think. If I can't think, I can't search for wisdom. So, I don't walk."

"Well," sighed Hobbes, "maybe some things other than wisdom are important, too."

"Yes," added Ms. Josie. "And maybe if you spend all your time searching for wisdom, you'll never find it."

"Yes," agreed Hobbes. "Maybe doing other things once in a while will help you think better when you are searching for wisdom. You could take a walk and *then* think about what you did."

"Besides," said Ms. Josie, "who says you can't think and walk at the same time? Have you ever tried?"

"Well . . . ," muttered Phrawg. "Well . . . ummm . . . I, ahhh . . . ."

"You haven't even *tried*, have you?" said Hobbes and Ms. Josie together.

"No," said Phrawg very softly. "I guess I haven't."

"Why not?" asked Ms. Josie.

"You're asking so many questions," said Phrawg, "that I need to take a minute to think about them. Let me shut my eyes so that I can concentrate."

Phrawg shut his eyes so that he could think really hard. "Can I do two things at the same time? I've been talking with Hobbes and Ms. Josie. Was I thinking then, too? If I wasn't thinking when I was talking, how could I know what I was saying? But I remember what I was saying. So, maybe I can do two things at once. But thinking and talking are so much alike. I still think I can't walk and think at the same time."

"No," said Phrawg. "Walking and thinking are so different from each other that I'm sure I can't do both at the same time."

"Well," insisted Hobbes, "I can."

"So can I," agreed Ms. Josie. "Come with us and we'll show you."

Phrawg started to move, but then stopped. "No, I can't."

"You can't *what?*" asked Hobbes.

"I can't walk," cried Phrawg.

"Sure you can," coaxed Ms. Josie. "It's been a long time, but you can do it. We'll help you."

"But you and Hobbes are so graceful when you walk," said Phrawg. "I can't walk like that. Phrawgs only jump."

"What's the matter with jumping?" asked Hobbes. "Phrawgs can jump forward, backward, sideways, up and down, any which way they want to."

"That's true," said Phrawg. "But it's all so awkward, especially compared with you and Ms. Josie. You can walk and run—and jump. It's all so smooth and beautiful."

"But we're cats," said Ms. Josie. "That's how we're supposed to move. You're a phrawg, and phrawgs are supposed to jump about."

"Yes," said Hobbes. "That's graceful, too. If I were a phrawg, that's just what I'd do. In fact, I'd jump as high and far as I could. That would be fun."

"What if *cats* jumped around like phrawgs?" asked Ms. Josie. "Wouldn't they look as funny as phrawgs walking around like cats?"

"You think that phrawgs would look silly walking around like cats?" replied Phrawg.

"Just imagine a phrawg slinking around the corner, waiting to pounce on mouse or running around the house trying to catch it," yowled Hobbes.

"Or just imagine a cat bounding around the house like a phrawg, trying to catch a mouse," howled Phrawg.

Hobbes, Ms. Josie, and Phrawg began laughing so hard that they shut their eyes and rolled around on the couch until all three fell to the floor. Phrawg quickly jumped back on the couch, opened his eyes, and saw Hobbes and Ms. Josie walking away from the couch.

"Wait! Wait!" shouted Phrawg.

Hobbes and Ms. Josie were surprised to hear Phrawg shouting. They returned to the couch to see what he wanted.

"Okay," he said, "now I've moved off the couch and jumped back up. That wasn't so bad. Maybe I will take a walk with you, after all."

"You haven't moved at all," said Ms. Josie. "You fell asleep for so long that we decided to take a walk by ourselves."

"I've been asleep?" asked Phrawg.

"Yes," said Hobbes. "And if you think I snore, you should hear yourself. I'll bet the giants would have heard you if they'd been here."

"So, I didn't really fall off the couch and jump back up?" asked Phrawg.

"No, you must have been dreaming," said Ms. Josie.

"But that's two things at once," said Hobbes. "Dreaming and snoring. So, come on, let's walk and talk."

"And think," said Ms. Josie.

Phrawg thought for a moment about jumping off the couch, but he paused to think some more. "This is all so confusing," he said. "Come back tomorrow. I need a little more time to think about this. Maybe I'll join you for a walk then." Soon he was sound asleep.

93

To order more copies of

Phrawg Phables: Wonderings and Wanderings

Each softcover copy is $10.00 with 25% discount for 10 or more copies.

\# copies _____ @ _____   = $_____

Shipping and Handling:
> $3.00 for first book and
> $1.00 for each additional book $_____

Tax: Michigan residents,
>   Add 6% sales tax $_____

Total   **$**_____

Make checks payable to Michael Pritchard.

Send order form with check to:

Michael Pritchard
2708 Ridgeview Dr.
Kalamazoo, MI 49008

Name_____

Street _____

City, State_____

Zip _____ Phone _____

Email _____